The
Mountain
and
Me

Annie Louise Twitchell

Brilliant.

The sky overhead is flooded with stars.
Over my mountain, Orion glistens.

I am safe here in the cradle of my world.

I am safe.

I am.

Far away, so dim I can barely see it, my town rests under the soft white clouds.

I've never lived outside of these streets and houses. For so long these boundaries have defined my world. A cage made of home.

There is no longer a cage.

The world spreads before me and I choose to come home.

.

Survival is not who I am.
Survival is what I did.

When you speak of me, call me by my name.

The air is clear and fresh above the trees.
I stand for a moment and look out,
remembering the last time I stood here.

All of the people I have been,
all of the ghosts of my past,
are here in the ashes in my hands.

I open my hands and let them go.

The wind sweeps them away and carries them off,
out of my reach.

I cannot bring them back.
I cannot change them.

I don't need to.

I am here, now, in the present.

I let go of my past and let the tears fall.

breathe.

you are enough.

the world would continue to spin if you were not here,
but a thing of beauty would be lost.

beauty, joy, love

these are the flowers that make the long journey
worth the trouble.

The water sings.

From the mountain peak it runs down to Norton Brook.

From the brook to Rapid Stream and from Rapid into the
Carrabassett River.

The Carrabassett meets the Kennebec and the Kennebec
runs into the Atlantic and the Atlantic brushes the other
oceans of the world.

I stand in the stream and the water rushes around me.

I am part of humanity, and humanity is part of me.

I am part of this world and this world is part of me.

I am Earth and Earth is me.

I am infinite and miniscule.

I am.

The simple kindness that I show so readily to others feels impossible to extend towards myself.

I feel other—separate—different. I do not think of myself the same as I think of my neighbor.

I have always been taught to love my neighbor as I love myself, but this summer—this year—I am faced with the lesson of learning to love myself as I love my neighbor.

I am learning.

There is always space to learn. There is always space to love.

And when it feels too hard, I come back to the mountains.

She's always there.

For every adventure and every disaster,
every heartbreak and every reunion.

She's always there.

She reminds me to treat this world with gentle hands.

To touch it with reverence.

To respect the world that knows me.

Mt. Abram
June 13, 2021

Today is my twenty-fourth birthday. Cricket and I left shortly after dawn and went to hike my mountain.

We spent almost eleven hours on the mountain and it was both the best and hardest day I've had in a long time.

The last time I was here, I was twelve. That was half my lifetime ago, and it was before all the bad things happened.

Last night I wrote out everything bad—everything—from the last twelve years. I wrote it out and then I burned the papers and collected the ashes in a bag. I carried all those ghosts of myself with me up the mountain.

I sprinkled the ashes on the wind at the tree line.

Watched the wind carry off the ghosts of myself until there was nothing left but my skin and the tears trickling down my cheeks.

I felt as though I was standing with the child I was before.

The child who climbed this mountain twelve years ago had no idea what her future held. She was full of life and she felt like she could conquer the world.

I lost that feeling somewhere along the way, but I realized I had it again as I stood there today.

When I see the mountains, I feel like I'm coming home.

This is my world.

There is enough space here for my body and for my soul.

I imagine that heaven is like my mountains.
The journey is hard sometimes but when you first reach the
tree line and see paradise stretched out at your feet, you
forget all the sweat and tears and the blister on your heel.

You forget about the miles behind you except to think that it
was all worth it.

There are many things I do not know about life, and about
God, and about heaven.

There are two things that I do know.

I am loved beyond comprehension, and at the end of this
life, at the end of this journey, I'm going home.

For now, for right here, that is enough.

ANNIE LOUISE TWITCHELL is a writer, poet, artist, and journalist in Western Maine. When she's not writing, she can often be found reading to her cats and houseplants, or wandering barefoot in the woods in search of dragons, fairies, and fireflies.

Connect with Annie Louise Twitchell at:

AnnieLouiseTwitchell.com
Facebook.com/AnnieLouiseTwitchell
Instagram: @the_bookish_cat_dragon
Twitter: AnnieTwitchell

Made in the USA
Middletown, DE
13 August 2023

36215041R00018